Easy to Use Frames to Adapt, Adopt and Apply to Your Content

POWERFUL
PRESENTATIONS

Volume One

39 Quick **OPENERS**, **PUZZLERS** and *ENERGIZERS*
that Spark Interest and Anchor Your Topic

Bob Pike CSP, CPAE and
Betsy Allen MBA, CSP, CMC

POWERFUL PRESENTATIONS

Volume One

PUBLISHER
The Bob Pike Group
7620 W. 78th St, Edina MN 55439

ISBN-10: 1-56447-038-5
ISBN-13: 978-1-56447-038-6

PRINTED IN THE U.S.A.
www.bobpikegroup.com

Table of Contents

Preface

In 451 BC, Confucius said, "What I hear, I forget; what I see, I remember; but what I do, I understand." This book, as is true of all the books we've written on presentations and training, is based on the premise that the more we involve people in our presentations, the more they'll remember and the more likely they will be to act on what they've seen, heard and experienced.

That's the goal of this new volume—to provide you with powerful, easy-to-use templates that you can drop your content into and create compelling involvement between your audience and your content. This book can certainly be read cover to cover – and if you choose that method then be sure to use a highlighter and some tape flags to mark activities you can use now – and those that you readily see have future value.

Don't be afraid, though, to use this as a cookbook. If you're making an entrée, you don't read the entire cookbook – you simply go to the entree section. So if you're looking for a visual puzzler, check out the table of contents, and feel free to jump around.

Remember, too, that one of the most important points is that whatever you do, it must relate to both your audience and your content. When everything you do is relevant, you'll get little or no push back about the audience being asked to participate. So press on, read on, and enjoy, but most importantly – use what you find on these pages.

Introduction

Imagine you start your presentation and enjoy the attention of your audience. It is so quiet, you can hear the click of your wireless mouse advancing your slide. All eyes are on you and your slides. They're watching, they're nodding, they're listening... or are they? You know they are in the room physically, yet how do you know they are in the room mentally?

Why use Openers, Puzzlers and Energizers?

Most presenters and trainers rarely, if ever, open a presentation; they just start. They rarely close with anchoring their main point; they just end. They rarely keep their participants energized once they've begun a presentation. Yet, the research is out: Sleep Learning doesn't work; involvement does. Failing to open, energize and close is an unprescribed sleeping pill to which this book is the antidote.

In the context of training, the purpose of a presentation is to transfer knowledge, build skills, and increase the confidence and desire of the participants to apply the knowledge and skills on their jobs. Why? So that they improve the performance they give or the results they get. However, if people are simply physically present, but not mentally present, your presentation is largely wasted. The frames you'll find in this volume can be filled with your content and used to get people focused and keep them energized as you engage them in your presentation.

When to use Openers, Puzzlers and Energizers?

Obviously, use a thought-provoking or eye-catching frame at the beginning of your presentation, but also use these as you transition from one topic to another or take a break. As you feel the group losing energy and want to involve them, try an energizer from this volume. That's why these have been designed to be done in as little as 60 seconds.

How do I customize this to my content?

Here are four simple steps for making sure that each activity you use fits your content:
1. Walk through the activity exactly as-is so you get a feel for the flow.
2. Think through the learning points the activity makes as it is written.
3. Ask yourself this question: will this learning point fit my presentation? If it does, you're home free. Use it in this form. If not, then go to the next step.
4. How could I adapt and adopt this activity (insert my content words, numbers or learning points) so that I can apply it for my purposes?

With many of the activities, you'll find suggested ways to look at the activity differently in order to adjust it to your content. In addition to building several of these into your presentation, get two or three additional ones ready so that if you need them, you can insert them in the moment.

VERBAL VISUAL NUMERICAL

1. Hangman

Set-up Script

Ready for a challenge? Remember hangman? You guess the letters and start to fill in the ones that are correct. In this case, the missing letters are in the beginning and end of the word – and the letters happen to be identical – the same three letters in the same order. What are they? Show the puzzle and pause.

Debrief & Adapt, Adopt and Apply (AAA) Possibilities

Power of Openings and Closings
The opening and closing of any training, presentation or sales call is the most important real estate owned. How you open and how you close will be remembered disproportionately to anything in-between.

Change, Learning and Perspective
You will never look at the word "underground" the same way again. My goal is that you will never look at (insert whatever you are teaching) the same way again when we are done here.

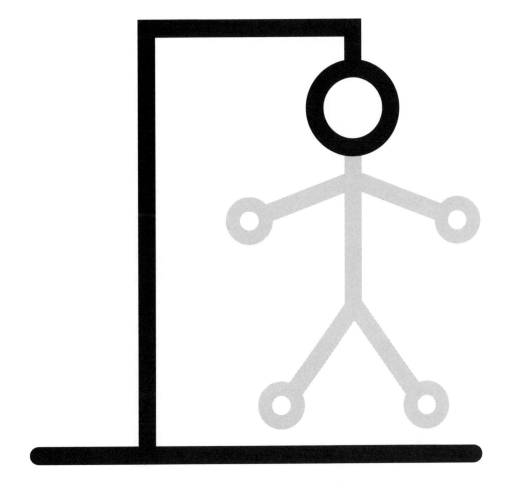

_ _ _ _ _ ergro _ _ _

VERBAL **VISUAL** **NUMERICAL**

2. The Root

Set-up Script

The blanks on this page can be filled in with words, all of which include the term "arm." See how many you can solve.

Debrief and AAA Possibilities

Use this to stress to the audience that you plan to "arm" them with the tools they need to be successful at what you are training. We use it for presentation platform skills. You could use it for operating a machine, running a camera, or using a software program.

Note that the words could either relate to what you're training or the stem ("arm" in this case) you choose could relate to your training. Note that there are prefixes and suffixes that are used frequently to make up your own (aim, ion, deed, etc.)

A particular quality that attracts; a delightful characteristic:

_ _ _arm

The art of preparing and dispensing drugs:

_ _ _arm_ _ _ _ _

To deprive of the means of attack or defense; render harmless:

_ _ _ _arm

The weapons and supplies of war with which a military unit is equipped:

arm_ _ _ _ _ _

VERBAL   VISUAL   NUMERICAL

3. Odd Man Out

Set-up Script

Imagine you are training new bank tellers.
Which of the following words does not belong with the other words
and why?

Hint: The solution relates to things that a teller needs to keep in mind when interacting with customers.

Debrief and AAA ideas

The two words (seen vertically at the beginning and ending of each of the horizontal words) can relate to your topic. Naturally, one or the other could relate to your content, a goal you're going to help them with or a problem you are going to solve.

You can make the point using the words and stress the need to stretch their thinking beyond the obvious during your talk or presentation.

pacific

radio

inventor

believe

valor

adaptive

tactic

edit

VERBAL   **VISUAL**   NUMERICAL

4. Perception is Reality – or Is It?

Set-up Script

In front of you is a cube with a dot in it. Where do you see the dot first? Where else can you see it? How many places can you see it?

Debrief and AAA Possibilities

Vision

Do you see the dot inside the cube in one place or in several? If you asked five people in your organization what their vision was, would you get five different answers? Would there be value in everyone having the same picture of the vision?

Resistance to change

When debriefing, you can ask how many people had trouble seeing the dot anywhere else without going back to seeing it in the original place. This is common and can be tied to our resistance to change (due to habit, comfort, etc.).

Problem Solving

Some people come to a meeting committed to a solution, not committed to solving a problem. They're like the ones who can see the dot in only one place. Others come committed to solving the problem. They often more readily see multiple options.

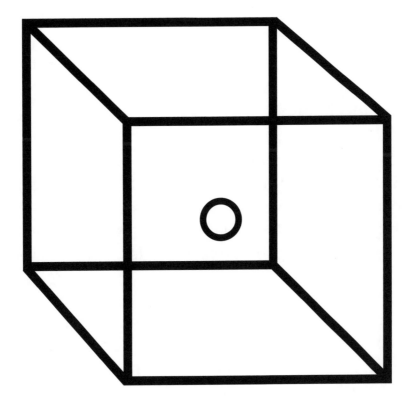

Can you see the dot?
How many places?

VERBAL   VISUAL   **NUMERICAL**

5. Me and My Niece

Set-up Script

Sometimes relationships change. Solve the query on the right page.

Debrief and AAA Possibilities

The Numbers

Many different points can be derived from this puzzle relating to the actual numbers (4, 28, or 48) which might be statistics, steps in a process, or a promised number of ideas. We use it to say you will learn four times as much from each other as you'll ever learn from the instructors to honor the expertise in the room and prepare the learners for an interactive session.

Problem Solving

Once solved, ask participants how solving this logic puzzle was like problem-solving at their company. You'll receive answers like: trial and error, looking for the easy way, stopping once they had "an answer" without looking for the "second" right answer, etc.

Process Improvement

Knowing "the answer" is one thing. Understanding "the process," which can give you the answer, is another. Go for understanding the process, not just the answer.

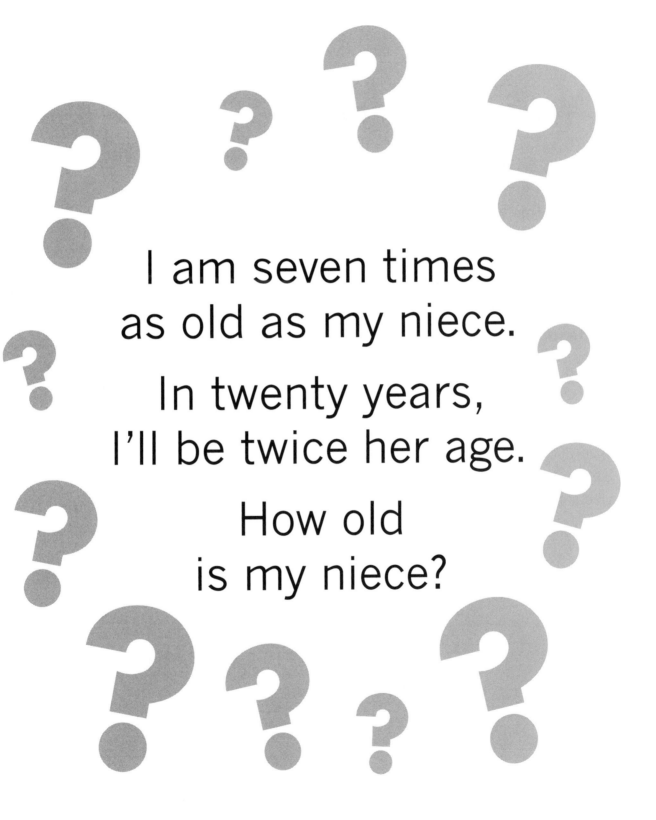

I am seven times
as old as my niece.

In twenty years,
I'll be twice her age.

How old
is my niece?

6. The End of the Road

Set-up Script

On the opposite page is a riddle and a puzzle wrapped into one.
What is "this" at the end of the road?

Debrief and AAA Possibilities

You could use this riddle as it is to open any lesson regarding "variety" which is the solution to the puzzle. Yet, you could rewrite the shell of the riddle to relate to any content you are teaching that you don't want people to miss.

Here is another example if the point you are making is "revisiting."

Content moves from short-term to long-term
When you do this the sixth time.
Before that, it is rarely firm.
Use different methods to give a feedback sign.

In a training class, this you want to use.
This keeps participants engaged and not asleep.
To repeat the same activity represents abuse.
Recognize through this, retention you will reap.

_ _ _ _ _ _ _ _ _y

VERBAL **VISUAL** NUMERICAL

7. Point of View

Set-up Script

Duplicate the drawing on the right on chart paper.

Place your forefingers on each end of the longest line and say: "Is it fair to say that this ..." move your forefingers to each end of the shortest line and say, "is taller than this?"

Repeat the movement, then ask: "Would it always be?"

Debrief and AAA Possibilities

Perspective
The answer you are looking for is "no." It depends on your perspective. They would all be the same length if you were looking at telephone poles down a country road. This could transition to or open any topic where you want people to keep multiple perspectives in mind, stretch their thinking or think creatively.

Experience
How you solve problems or meet change depends on where you have been and what experience you bring to the issue.

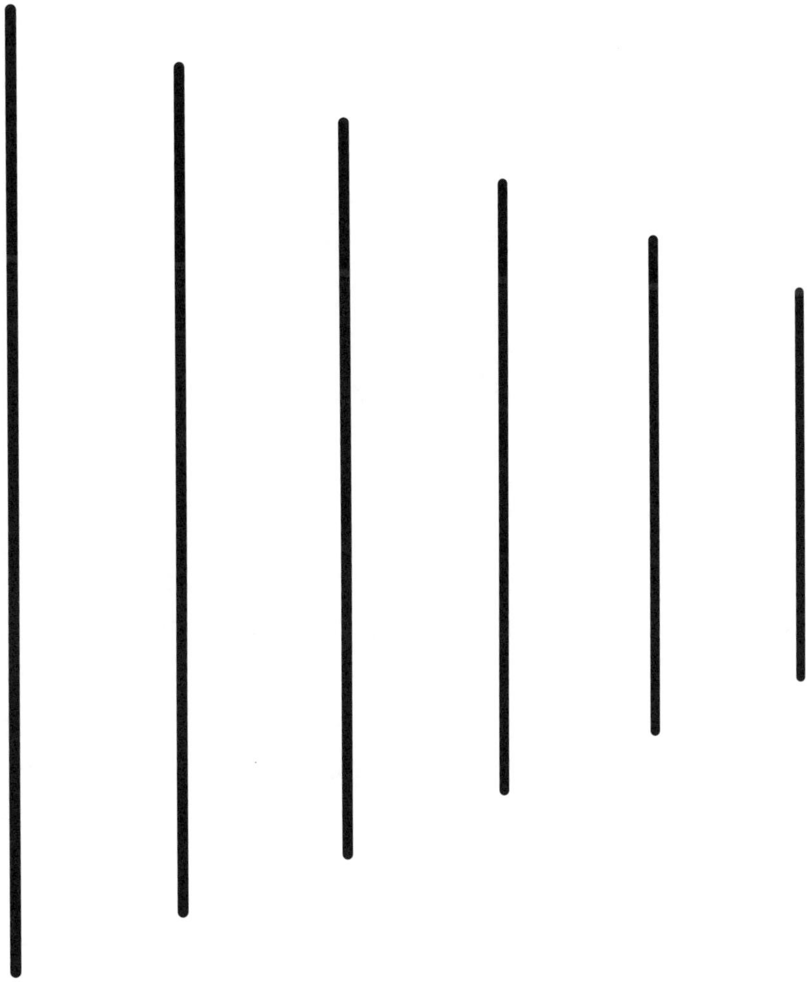

8. Medical Wuzzle

Set-up Script

Pretend you are training doctors or medical professionals of any kind.

These are wuzzles, which is a graphic play on words. Starting with "broken bones" in the upper left hand corner of this page of wuzzles, solve as many as you can.

Hint: Vocalizing possible solutions may help you find the solution more quickly.

Debrief and AAA Possibilities

This could open any lesson where you want the experts to participate, share best practices, stretch their thinking, look at things from all angles, etc.

This puzzler might stump them and prepare them for new learning. Wuzzles are a great way to introduce objectives or organize key learning.

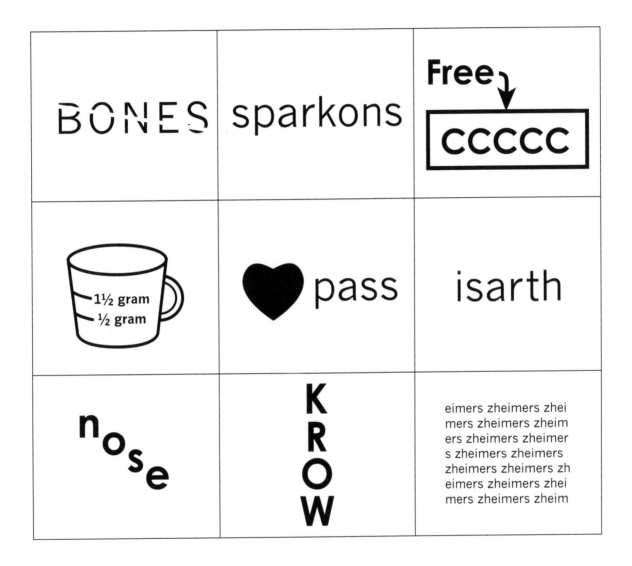

VERBAL   VISUAL   NUMERICAL

9. Even-ing the Load

Set-up Script

Duplicate the puzzler on chart paper and ask the question, "How many tasks were assigned to begin with?"

Debrief and AAA Possibilities

This could open a discussion of the need for attention to detail, deductive versus inductive reasoning, problem solving, consulting, making assumptions, etc.

You could also create the puzzle to reveal numbers which have a purpose to your content such as steps in a process, significant statistic or days to completion.

If you do one of my tasks, we have an even number; yet if I do one of yours, I will have five times the tasks assigned to you.

How many tasks do you and I have to begin with?

VERBAL VISUAL NUMERICAL

10. Seeing is Not Remembering

Set-up Script

Pair up participants standing and facing each other. Show the money.
Ask each pair of partners to produce a $20 bill. If any of the pairs cannot find a $20 bill, lend them one or ask them to use any other bill. Ask the partners to hold a single bill by its top corners. Each participant can see only one side of the bill. Ask partners to take turns asking these questions about their side of the bill when the question applies.

Whose portrait is on my side?
Which direction is the portrait facing?
How many times is the number 20 printed on my side?
Is there a bird on my side? Which one?
How many digits does the serial number have?
What words, other than "twenty," are on both sides?

Ask the questions that time allows.
As soon as one partner asks the question, the other partner must answer (and of course they are not looking at the side of the bill which has the answer). Correct answers earn a point. Incorrect answers or no answers earn no points. The questioner should immediately give the correct answer.

Debrief and AAA Possibilities

Ask your audience to discuss how familiarity breeds mindlessness.
What work-related supplies and tools do we take for granted?
What could we gain by paying attention to these objects and people?
Say to participants, "There are at least three learning points that can be drawn from this activity that apply to our topic of (fill in the blank) – take one minute with your group to brainstorm what they are."

1. How can you stand behind someone when he or she stands behind you?

2. What looks like a rhinoceros, moves like a rhinoceros, and is as big as a rhinoceros, but weighs nothing?

3. John's mother had three children. One was named April. One was named May. What was the third one named?

4. What multiplies by division?

5. Why are there so many Joneses in the phone directory?

VERBAL · VISUAL · NUMERICAL

12. Your Ear Knows

Set-up Script

Pretend you are training pharmaceutical representatives or medical professionals of any kind. Once they have the puzzle (either projected or on chart paper), ask which Margaret likes doing: writing scripts or giving samples and why?

Debrief and AAA Possibilities

In this frame, you could use words from any industry and relate to attention to detail, more than one right answer, creative thinking and problem solving.

Hint: Where are the silent letters?

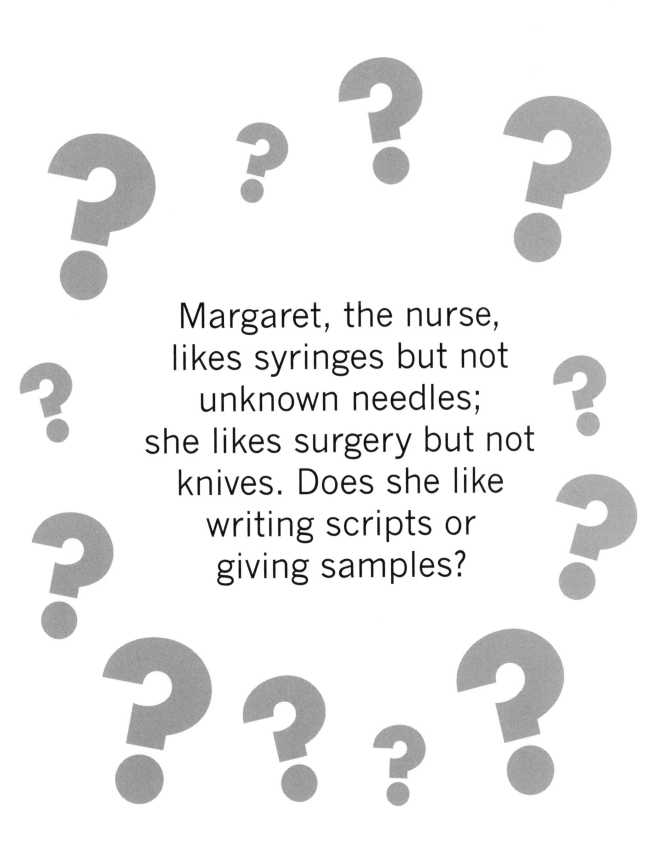

Margaret, the nurse, likes syringes but not unknown needles; she likes surgery but not knives. Does she like writing scripts or giving samples?

13. Alphabet Answer

Set-up Script

Once your participants have this puzzle (either projected or on chart paper), ask, "One of the things we don't want to say in training is 'Let's _____.' What word fills the blank?"

This word is described letter by letter in this poem. What do we want to avoid saying in training?

Debrief and AAA Possibilities

This puzzle concept will work with minor changes for any six-letter word related to your training topic.

My first is in snarl but not in snail
My second in relate but not in tail
My third in veil but not in gown
My fourth in tiara not in crown
My fifth in tree you plainly see
My last in whole aids memory

Don't say, _____
"Let's _____."

14. Favorite Foods

Set-up Script

Pretend you work for the Kellogg Company.

Before you are five Kellogg Company products all run together with the vowels missing. They are assorted in groups of three consonants in order. Name the products if you can.

Debrief and AAA Possibilities

You can use this puzzle concept for a phrase, your products, competitor's products or anything related to your topic. Just decide what you wish to emphasize and remove the vowels and put the consonants in order in groups of three.

frs tdf lks ppt

rts crc krs spc

lkf rtt wst bls

VERBAL VISUAL NUMERICAL

15. Three Cheeses

Set-up Script

Pretend you are training farmers, chefs or pizza makers. You can use this puzzle as-is.

The names of three famous cheeses are interspersed on the opposite page. All the letters are in the correct order for each word but are mixed in with the other cheeses. Unscramble the letters.

Debrief and AAA Possibilities

This puzzle concept (inter-lettering or interspersing) could be used with any training topic. Just select what you wish to anchor, inter-letter the 3 to 5 words and voila!

What made this puzzle easy or difficult to solve?
What process did you use to find the answer?
How does this puzzle and process apply to our topic of (fill in the blank)?

RMOOCZQZHAREEUDEFLODARTLRA

VERBAL   **VISUAL**   **NUMERICAL**

16. Nothing from Something

Set-up Script

Rearrange these six toothpicks to make "nothing." No toothpick can be bent, broken or placed over another. You must use all six of the toothpicks.

Debrief and AAA Possibilities

With this and some of the other activities, you might want to appoint one person in each group to observe the process that the group uses to come up with a solution.

What were some things that made this task easy to solve?

What, if anything, got in the way?

What, if anything, could have made it easier?

How did the approach that you took either help or hinder finding a solution?

This could be used as-is to introduce a system, creative thinking, or problem-solving to name a few.

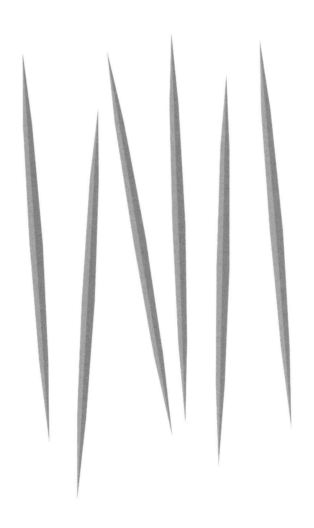

VERBAL   VISUAL   NUMERICAL

17. There But Not Seen

Set-up Script

Imagine you are working for a cell phone company and you are learning their products (three of which are Bluetooth, cell phone and case).

Three products that our cell phone company markets to customers are hidden in the sentences to your right—at least their names are. One or more names appear in each statement. Find the products.

Debrief and AAA Possibilities

Which product was easiest to find? Why?
Which was the most difficult? Why?
What is the significance of the words for today's topic?

Hide the name of anything in real or made-up sentences.

Before leaving under the awning outside, other guests gathered in the cellar to taste wine. Perhaps I should join them because I won't see them again for weeks.

VERBAL   **VISUAL**   **NUMERICAL**

18. Snake Walk

Set-up Script

The coiled sentence contains an idea that every trainer needs to recognize. Start at the right spot and move, letter by letter in any direction, to find the sentence. It starts with "sleep" and ends in "work."

Debrief and AAA Possibilities

Literally, any even-lettered, sentence, phrase or concept can be used in this puzzle concept.

What does this sentence have to do with our topic today?

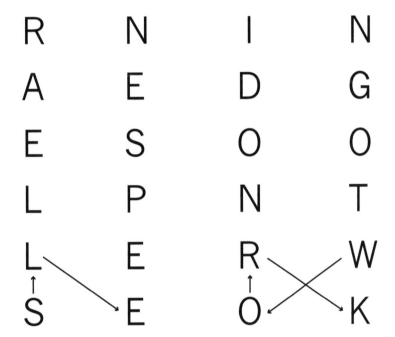

19. Common Content

Set-up Script

One letter can replace the first letter of each word pair shown below so that two new English words are formed. Place the letter you have used for both words on the line between the words.

(Example: rain_____ dark= Main <u>M</u> Mark)

Your goal, when finished, is to have the new letters spell out a new English word vertically that pertains to your topic.

Debrief and AAA Possibilities

What made this puzzle easy or difficult to solve?
Were some words more difficult than others? Which? Why?
What word did you find and how does it relate to today's topic?

This puzzle concept can be adapted to words related to your content. See if you can't create one with your topic be it safety or benefits or coaching. All you need is your word and perhaps a dictionary.

add _____ sat

dine _____ main

mast _____ darn

same _____ mail

bar _____ wager

link _____ bound

VERBAL VISUAL NUMERICAL

20. The Vowels Have It

Set-up Script

The following puzzle consists of a commitment we suggest all trainers make to each other with all the vowels removed. The remaining letters have been broken into groups of five. Put the vowels back in to find the commitment.

The clusters don't relate to the beginning or ending of the words.

Debrief and AAA Possibilities

Why would this be an important commitment to make?
How has your trainer demonstrated this commitment to you?
What are three ways you could demonstrate this going forward?

This puzzle concept can be adapted to most phrases related to your content. Choose your topic, remove the vowels and put the remaining consonants in clusters of five.

Itsbt hgdnt hsdnt thsgn thstg

21. Consonant Comments

Set-up Script

If Iowa is west of the Mississippi River, cross out all the W's and X's. If not, cross out all the E's. If we remember less of what we hear than what we say, cross out all the P's and Q's. If we remember less of what we say than what we hear, cross out all the R's. If we remember less of what we read than what we hear and see, cross out the O's and J's. If not, cross out the I's and G's.

What word is left which is an essential ingredient to participant-centered training?

Debrief and AAA Possibilities

This can be used to open a topic, revisit a couple truths quickly or close a lesson.

A variation would be to give some participants written instructions and others the verbal instructions. Then ask which instructions were easier to follow. Why?

WEPNWEPJRXGOIQZXOEQRWS

VERBAL   VISUAL   **NUMERICAL**

22. The Case of the Missing Numbers

Set-up Script

This addition puzzle uses letters instead of numbers. Each letter must be replaced with a number—the same number each time the letter appears. The puzzle will then be correct mathematically.

Debrief and AAA Possibilities

This puzzle can represent the XX (solution) ideas from your training that will be available for the participants to adapt, adopt and apply. It could also be rewritten to cleverly total any number, statistic, or little known fact you want to emphasize.

As an alternative, you might have some people work together to solve the puzzle and some work separately. You might also want an observer to document the process that those working together used to solve the puzzle.

Some debrief questions might be:
1. Was it easier solving the puzzle together or alone? What reasons could you give?
2. Did time pressure have anything to do with solving the puzzle?
3. What process was used to find a solution?
4. When a solution was found, did anyone volunteer to help others find the solution? Why or why not?
5. In what ways does this activity mirror what happens on the job?
6. If you had it to do over again, what guidelines would you put in place to help find the solution more easily?
7. How could these same guidelines be modified to help you get the most from this seminar?

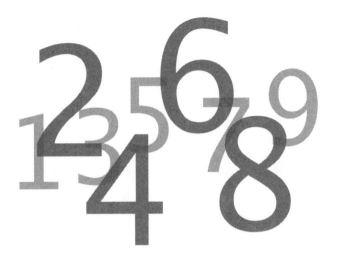

OH

OH

OH

+ OH
_____

NO?

VERBAL VISUAL **NUMERICAL**

23. Grammar Math

Set-up Script

How much is "Jessica" worth using the same system?

Debrief and AAA Possibilities

What are the various methods you used before arriving at a solution?
What does stretching your thinking have to do with (name of your topic)?
How does having a process or approach to use simplify solving problems?
What are the steps in the system we are about to learn?

Bob is 5, Arabella is 20, while Betsy and Tina are 10.

VERBAL   VISUAL   **NUMERICAL**

24. Crack the Code

Set-up Script

Cracking a system when you know the code is easy. Look at the code on the opposite page. Which two numbers are next in the series of code? Choose from the answers below.

A. 8 2   B. 9 2   C. 3 8   D. 2 7

Debrief and AAA Possibilities

You could use the puzzle as-is to open a systems training.

Introduce or reinforce a system or the use of discipline with this puzzle.

Alternatively, the purpose of the puzzle could be to find the number 82 or any number which represents a valuable statistic, number in a sequence or ideas to take away from your seminar.

1 5 9 2 6 8 3 7 7 4 8 6 5 9 5 6 10 4 7 9 3 8 __ __

VERBAL VISUAL NUMERICAL

25. Crack the Code[2]

Set-up Script

Cracking a system when you know the code is easy. Look at the code on the opposite page. Hidden in the code are two things especially important to interactive learning. Which two letters complete the code? Choose from the selections below then discover two keys to interactive learning.

Which is next in the series which hides two things especially important to interactive learning?

EF   RE   ED   EE

Debrief and AAA Possibilities

Use new vocabulary words that you'd like participants to start to memorize. Use words inter-lettered going forward or backward with this speedy puzzle. You could also use this activity to revisit important vocabulary and transition to other content.

Either way, you open the way to deductive logic and lateral thinking.

2

ESXRPEEZRIIGERNECN_ _

VERBAL

VISUAL

NUMERICAL

26. Toothpick Tangle

Set-up Script

Rearrange these nine toothpicks by touching only two, to make a correct equation (there may be several solutions).

Once you have a solution, put the toothpicks back as shown and find another right answer.

Debrief and AAA Possibilities

The lesson here could be the value of looking for two right answers to truly see the problem. It also illustrates how hard it is to change perspective and not see your original solution.

VERBAL **VISUAL** NUMERICAL

27. Center This!

Set-up Script

The diagram has eight sections. Each of them contains five letters with a question mark in the middle showing that one letter is missing. Your job is to find the one letter that is missing and then rearrange the letters in each section to form eight words. All the words relate to participant-centered training.

Debrief and AAA Possibilities

Obviously, these eight words relate to our topic of participant-centered training. Yet, you could use any eight words of the same length with one letter in common relating to your topic.

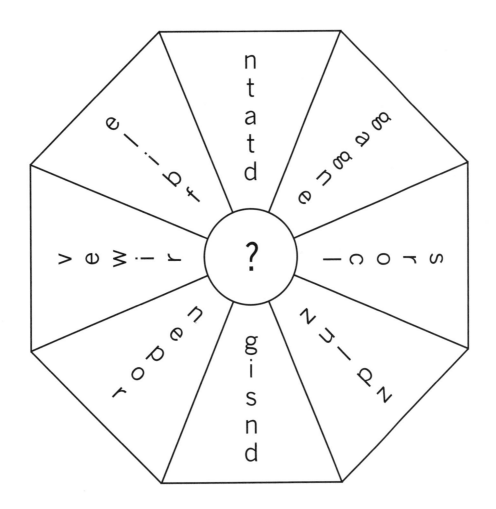

28. Starting Right

Set-up Script

Complete the last square of letters using the same system as followed in the previous four squares. The sentence describes an important need of participant-centered training.

Debrief and AAA Possibilities

Once solved, ask participants to brainstorm how they solved the puzzle.
What process did they use?
How does that process relate to our topic today?

The sentence can be any sentence, truth or falsehood related to your topic. The lesson could also be related to systems, creativity or higher order cognition.

O	P
	E
E	N

R	S
	E
B	R

A	K
	E
P	R

O	C
	P
C	U

A	T
	?
I	O

VERBAL   VISUAL   NUMERICAL

29. What Day is It?

Set-up Script

The trainer posted this notice outside the classroom door.
What day does the class meet again?

Debrief and AAA Possibilities

What was frustrating about solving this riddle?

Think of a time that you received an email or communication of any type that said something simple in an overly complicated way?

What can we do to simplify our communication?

What makes email a particularly challenging way to communicate?

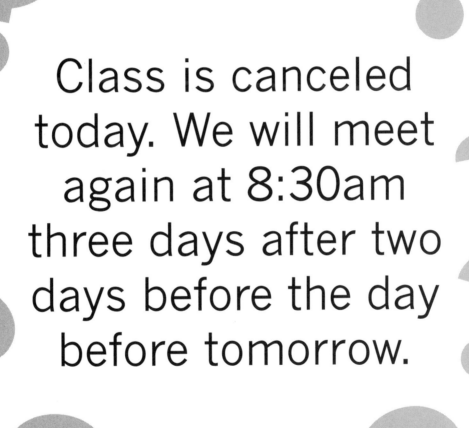

Class is canceled today. We will meet again at 8:30am three days after two days before the day before tomorrow.

30. Message in a Circle

Set-up Script

What is the word coiled in the circle?

Debrief and AAA Possibilities

The long coiled word can be anything related to your training or a transition from one topic to the next.

The coiled word or sentence could also be posted at the front of the room as your audience is entering to spark curiosity and interest in your topic.

REINFORCEMENT

VERBAL   VISUAL   NUMERICAL

31. Squared

Set-up Script

A particular process has been consistently used to determine the middle number in the pattern. Fill in the missing number.

Debrief and AAA Possibilities

This puzzle can be used to arrive at a particular number, open a system or project planning session and make the point that by working together we'll exponentially increase our results!

3   2

121

3   3

---

18   19

6084

20   21

---

1   1

?

1   1

32. Bridge Words

Set-up Script

In each of the word pairs in the puzzle opposite, a different word can be placed between the two words on the line to make two new words.

See the dashes in between to indicate the number of letters you are looking for in each word. Each word relates to a training class in person or online.

What are the five words?

Debrief and AAA Possibilities

This puzzle can be customized to any topic, industry or company with commonly used words or combinations.

cross __ __ __ __ __ search

work __ __ __ __ __ worm

flip __ __ __ __ __ __ __ paper

on __ __ __ __ __ up

class __ __ __ __ __ set up

33. Down and Across

Set-up Script

If you stack the words that match these definitions, you will have a word square that reads the same across and down (periods count).

Debrief and AAA Possibilities

Use this puzzle to open a lesson on needs assessment with one answer making the key point that you want to uncover "real" and perceived needs.

This puzzle can be customized to any topic, industry or company with commonly used words or combinations.

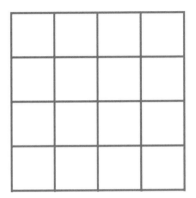

1. A member of a feudal class
   of people in Europe owned by a lord

2. At all times; always

3. Uncover these and perceived needs

4. *abbr.* Fräulein

VERBAL   VISUAL   NUMERICAL

34. Twisted Topic

Set-up Script

The twisted sentence opposite can be unscrambled by finding the right letter for a start and then tracing letter by letter up, down, sideways or diagonally to find a statement. (There will be one null letter X.)

The sentence regards the role of a training facilitator.

Hint: It starts with "Let us be ...

Debrief and AAA Possibilities

This puzzle can be customized to any topic, industry or company with commonly used sentences.

It could also point to the need to follow a system or expectation of performance so work goes quickly.

L U T T H E S S T

S E T O N E A E A

B U I O N D G H G

E G D E T I E T E

T H E H E S O N X

VERBAL | VISUAL | NUMERICAL

35. Elementary, My Dear Watson

Set-up Script

The puzzle opposite represents work (X) to be done equally by each of four employees. Find the way to divide the work by four so that the division is equal per employee, is identically shaped, and each employee area has six corners.

Debrief and AAA Possibilities

How did you find the solution?
How many different options did you try before solving?
What helped/hindered your ability to solve?

The "L" shape of the solution suggests the need to be creative to solve some problems and look for many approaches before settling on the best.

X		X		X
	X		X	
X				X
	X		X	
X		X		X

VERBAL ★ **VISUAL** NUMERICAL

36. Triad Triangles

Set-up Script

Arrange nine toothpicks to make a triangle. Now use those same nine toothpicks to make five triangles.

Debrief and AAA Possibilities

What kind of thinking did this puzzle require?

This puzzle is about stretching your thinking so that you include upside down and right side up triangles. This requires lateral thinking (sideways).

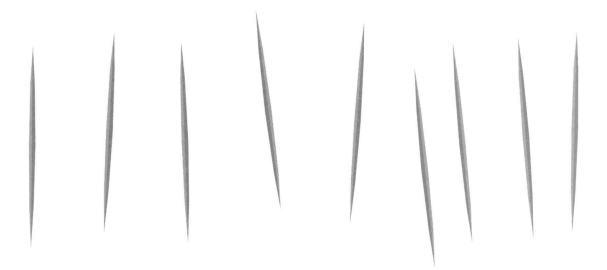

VERBAL VISUAL NUMERICAL

37. Steal This!

Set-up Script

Why is the man scared to go home?
What else is happening?

Debrief and AAA Possibilities

What assumptions did you find yourself making? Gather ideas.
You often get variations on the following which lead to some intriguing discussion.
Home is a structure. In this sentence, home is actually home plate.
Afraid in this case is not fear for safety; it is the fear of not reaching home because of being called out by the guy with the mask. We assume fear is teeth chattering, scared of bodily harm.
Mask is often assumed to be altering or hiding appearance or something psychological, but in this case, it is for protection.

Used as-is, this could make the point that we need deliberate effort and thought to get beyond our existing paradigms. Consider creating your own misleading statement using company jargon that, without explanation, would mean something very different.

Alternative

You could teach who, what, where, why, and how questioning skills. For this version, they get a certain amount of yes or no questions. We waste our questions by repeatedly asking the same question different ways and not listening well while other groups ask questions.

Contributed by Tricia Brainard

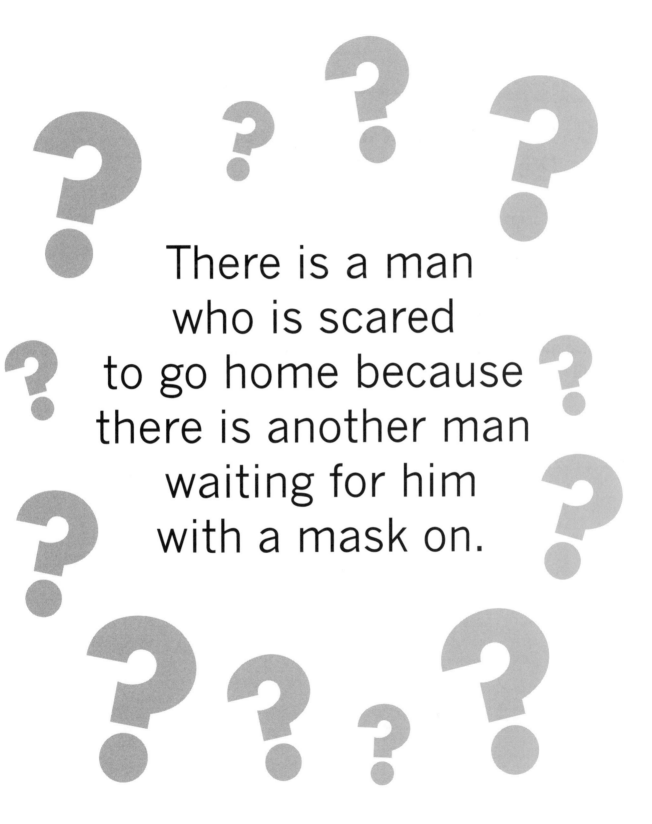

There is a man
who is scared
to go home because
there is another man
waiting for him
with a mask on.

VERBAL   VISUAL   NUMERICAL

38. It's Not What You Make; It's What You Take!

Set-up Script

Unscramble the top three words and use the circled letters to unscramble the final solution. This reveals a truth about the American Way.

Debrief and AAA Possibilities

This could be used as-is to introduce a finance class or changed to make any point you want regarding your content.

uvsgoserrene   ⊙ _ _ _ _   _ _ _ _ ⊙

tepofirnt   _ _ _ _   _ _ ⊙ _ ⊙

vrhoedae   _ _ _ _ _ ⊙ _

Net Profit or Discretionary Income is _ _ _ _ _ _

39. Mr. Greedy

Set-up Script

What did Andrea spend? Ask audiences to shout out their first reaction to this without giving them much time to think.

Debrief and AAA Possibilities

You might use this to open a financial topic as-is.

The first reaction might be that Andrea spent $.50 or $1.50. That's the way it is with numbers. On first glance, you might come up with an answer, yet through analysis discover another answer. Look further for the answer.

John and Andrea went
to the store with $2.50
to buy candy. They walked
out broke. John spent a
$1.00 more than Andrea.

About the Authors

Bob Pike, CSP, CPAE

Chairman/CEO, The Bob Pike Group
Founder/Editor-in-Chief—
Creative Training Techniques newsletter
Chairman, Executive Board—Lead Like Jesus

Bob has been developing, marketing, training and consulting on training and human performance improvement since 1969. In that time, he has designed and delivered over 600 training programs of one day or longer for clients like IBM, Pfizer, Hewlett Packard, Vanderbilt University, and ATT.

In 1987, he founded the *Creative Training Techniques* newsletter, the most widely read in the field. He has written or served as editor of more than 21 books in the field and created more than a dozen video programs, including one for the BBC entitled "Creative Training and Presentation Techniques" which won the best business-to-business video series award.

He has served on the national or international Board of Directors for the American Society for Training and Development (ASTD), the National Speakers Association (NSA), and the International Alliance for Learning (IAL).

An outstanding speaker and trainer, he has keynoted at major conferences around the world for more than 25 years. Since 1980, he has been one of the top five rated presenters at ASTD's International Conference and Exposition.

Betsy Allen, MBA, CSP, CMC, MOK

Senior Vice President, The Bob Pike Group

Betsy has been consulting and training through seminars and keynotes for over 20 years. During that time, she has enjoyed adding value to clients like Wells Fargo, Merck, Caterpillar, GlaxoSmithKline, U.S. Marine Corps, government agencies, school systems and many more. Her Harvard MBA, entrepreneurial experience and success as a participant-centered, dynamic presenter led her to The Bob Pike Group. As senior vice president, she partners with clients on results-based integrated design, delivers train-the-trainer seminars and customized workshops to improve employee effectiveness, and enhance team performance and strategic alignment.

She has contributed to professional development by serving as founding president of the National Speakers Association local chapter of NSA Hawaii and president of the Hawaii Chapter of the American Society for Training and Development, and most recently Program Chair in Southwest Florida.

Solutions

1. "underground"

2. A particular quality that attracts; a delightful characteristic: **Charm**

   The art of preparing and dispensing drugs: **Pharmacy**

   To deprive of the means of attack or defense; render harmless: **Disarm**

   The weapons and supplies of war with which a military unit is equipped: **Armament**

3. Solution is Believe doesn't fit, because without it, the first letters spell "private" and the last letters "correct."

5. Four years old

6. Variety

8. From left to right: Broken Bones, Parkinsons, Frequency, Sonogram, Heart Bypass, Arthritis, Diagnose, Work up, Alzheimers

9. I start out with four and you with two.

11. 1. Stand back to back, 2. Shadow of a rhinoceros, 3. John, 4. An amoeba, 5. The families live in the city.

12. She likes giving samples; she does not like words with silent letters like "writing."

13. Let's review

14. Frosted Flakes, Poptarts, crackers, Special K, Fruit Twistables

15. Roquefort, Cheddar and Mozzarella

16. NIL or a hexagon zero

17. The three hidden products are Bluetooth, cell phone and case.

    Before **l**eaving **und**er **t**he awning **o**utside, **oth**er guests gathered in the **cell**ar to taste wine. **Per**haps I s**h**ould jo**in** t**h**em be**cause** I won't see them again for weeks.

18. Sleep Learning Doesn't Work

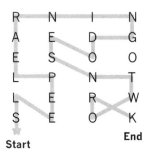

Start **End**

19. Opener

20. Let's be the Guide on the Side, not the Sage on the Stage.

21. ENERGIZERS

22. O=2, H=3, N=9, so 92 is the solution

23. **15**, 5 = each syllable is worth 5 points

24. **A. 8 2** The code is every fourth number descends, then the second number is ascending, then the third number ascends from five and then descends from 10.

25. **EE -** "Experience" is inter-lettered with "Energizers" backwards

26.

27. The missing letter is "E" in the following words: puzzle, design, opener, review, belief, attend, engage, closer

28. "N" completes the puzzle. "Openers break preoccupation" is written using the same pattern in each square (upper left, upper right, lower left, lower right then middle to spell your desired phrase).

29. Tomorrow

30. Reinforcement

31. **16,** the four numbers are added and then squared to get the middle number.

32. word, book, chart, line, room

33. serf
    ever
    real
    frl .

34. Let us be the guide on the side, not the sage on the stage

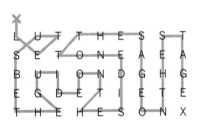

35.

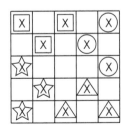

36.

37. The man is a baseball player trying to steal home and the mask is on the catcher who may tag the player and cause an out.

38. gross revenue, net profit and overhead as upper clues with "great" as final solution

39. Andrea spent $.75, $1.75 is what John spent.

About the Bob Pike Group

The Bob Pike Group has provided train-the-trainer workshops and consulting services to individuals and corporations for more than 30 years. Clients have been applying Bob's Participant-Centered Instructional System to build their learning organizations, strengthen retention and enrich desired results.

This comprehensive instructional system, complete with design, delivery and class management components, is now being applied to performance-based outcomes to strengthen the business relationship between the training department and the company's business objectives.

In addition to Bob Pike, a team of senior consultants with experience in a variety of industries and enterprises have been certified by Bob in his systems and processes. These consultants travel nationally and internationally conducting customized in-house training programs and providing consulting services for clients.

Clients have asked The Bob Pike Group to help move them from suspendible to strategic in their roles. Today's challenges demand bold action, common language and clear business metrics that measure results. All training directors and trainers must know how to elicit ownership organization-wide, create strategic partnerships and provide evidence of bottom line performance results.

If you would like to discuss any training or consulting topic in more detail or would like more information on The Bob Pike Group's public workshops or comprehensive system of performance solutions, visit www.BobPikeGroup.com or call (800) 383-9210.

"For the trainer that wants to move beyond lecture-base training, I recommend Bob Pike's participant-centered seminars and in-house consultants. Our staff has applied the ideas they've learned from Bob and his consultants to make the training we offer our clients more effective. Hundreds of other organizations do the same thing."
Ken Blanchard, Ph.D.
Co-Author of The One Minute Manager

Train-the-Trainer Boot Camp

- Learn to apply participant-centered techniques to improve the design and delivery of your training programs.
- Watch retention rates soar to **90%** or more with our special review and memory techniques.
- Acquire proven techniques and processes to design and deliver training in **25%** less time.
- Learn how to shrewdly use participant buy-in, accountability and personal action plans to help ensure transfer to the job with measurable results.
- Get the interaction dynamics of a small group even in sessions with several hundred attendees.
- Appeal to all adult learning styles.
- The most exciting, rewarding and immediately useful training "boot camp" you will ever attend!

"The Bob Pike's Train-the-Trainer Boot Camp was exceptional. I often refer back to the course material to help design and facilitate classes that get participants more engaged. The instructor was always supportive and best of all, modeled the concepts so we could see what the right behaviors and, skills looked like. I thought this was one of the best classes I have attended on facilitation skills and I have already recommended it to two co-workers."

Crystal Zunker, Sr. Talent Development Specialist,
RadioShack

Train-the-Trainer 101

New trainers and subject matter experts learn new skills and techniques to dramatically transform their presentation skills. It focuses on the basics of vocal, verbal and visual presentation;interactivity; body language; and delivery style. Use this knowledge to communicate more effectively, with better results.

The Bob Pike Group Website

We are your one-stop shop for consulting needs; but what if you need other resources? Books, creative tools and props, software for training program design, and more can be found in our online store. On our site, you'll also find article archives written by Bob and other BPG training consultants on creative training tips, graphic organizers, emergency training toolkit ideas and more. Visit us at www. BobPikeGroup.com and sign up for our free ezine.

To learn more about our public workshops, conference or in-house solutions, call (800) 383-9210 or visit www.BobPikeGroup.com.

Participant-Centered Results-Based Integrated Design

This visual, repeatable designing process starts with Don Kirkpatrick's Level IV evaluation and creates in reverse. Starting with stakeholder buy-in, purpose consensus, and metrics identified, this process transforms existing or creates new performance improvement efforts that change business. Field-tested and used repeatedly, BPG has assisted clients like Kellogg, Johnson & Johnson, AAA, Wells Fargo Business Credit, Honeywell and many others...

The Bob Pike Group's Annual Training Conference

This conference provides valuable information and an opportunity to improve skills for everyone in training – trainers, subject matter experts, content developers, senior trainers, training managers, business/performance consultants and training executives. The Bob Pike Group's consultants will be delivering their newest material as well as bringing back time-tested, valuable material that can be immediately applied.

To learn more about our public workshops, conference or in-house solutions, call (800) 383-9210 or visit www.bobpikegroup.com.

Research-Based Creative Teaching Strategies™ (RCTS)

Based on the Bob Pike Group Boot Camp principles, this Teach-the-Teacher workshop turns the focus away from lecture-based teaching toward instructor-led small group interaction and helps students adapt, adopt and apply what they learn.

Sales Autopsy Workshop

A Customized Suite of Strategies to Boost Performance
Designed for sales professionals and sales managers, this program shows how to increase sales by disqualifying early, spending time wisely and getting rid of the old-school sales rules. This approach builds on techniques introduced in the best-selling book *Sales Autopsy: 50 Postmortems Reveal What Killed the Sale (and what might have saved it)* by The Bob Pike Group trainer Dan Seidman.

Creative Training Techniques™ for Technical Trainers

A specialized workshop which models our unique participant-centered training strategies and applies them directly to technical content.

Creative Training Techniques™ for One-on-One or One-on-Few Trainers

This workshop helps trainers use proven components of effective classroom training within the unique one-on-one training scenario.

Instructional Design – A Results-Based Approach
Learn our proven process and framework for developing programs that ensure participants take the right knowledge, skills, and attitudes back to the job.

Performance Consulting
For new and aspiring performance consultants and training directors who have a stake when it comes to providing performance solutions, not just training programs.

Performance Coaching System
Our coaching system, featuring the Team Directory, includes a process and suite of materials for managers to use in helping direct reports succeed at a higher level. Using the Hartman-Kinsel thinking assessment, managers better understand the key motivators and attributes that have the greatest impact on the performance of their employees.

Visit www.BobPikeGroup.com for more information
or to sign up for our free monthly e-Zine.